God's Little Instruction Book
for Parents

Honor Books
Tulsa, Oklahoma

2nd Printing

God's Little Instruction Book for Parents
ISBN 1-56292-553-9
Copyright © 1999 by Honor Books
P.O. Box 55388
Tulsa, Oklahoma 74155

Introduction

Unfortunately, babies aren't delivered with instruction manuals. Parenting skills usually develop while heating bottles on sleepless nights, cleaning up after messy toddlers, and coaching Little League and soccer teams. A family's first child is usually the guinea pig, but by the time the third or fourth baby arrives, parenting is *almost* as natural as breathing.

Experience teaches us by trial and error, but God already has written a great manual for parenting success—the Bible. Inspired centuries ago by the best Father of all, the Word of God is packed with practical wisdom to help you become a better parent. God's Word is just as relevant today as it was when it was written centuries ago.

Honor Books is proud to offer you this collection of inspirational quotes and Scriptures to help you succeed in the world's most important profession—parenting. Keep this little power-packed volume handy to motivate you throughout the day. Learn to speak words of life to your children, and they will grow up to be a blessing to you and to others.

*T*he most important thing that parents
can teach their children is how to
get along without them.

———•◦•◦•———

Watch yourselves closely so that you do not forget the things
your eyes have seen or let them slip from your heart....
Teach them to your children and to their children after them.

—Deuteronomy 4:9

———•◦•◦•———

There are two great injustices that can befall a child: One is to punish him for something he didn't do. The other is to let him get away with something he knows is wrong.

The Lord is known by his justice.
—Psalm 9:16

5

$\mathcal{S}$top trying to perfect your child,
but keep trying to perfect your
relationship with him.

———◆◆◆———

A cheerful look brings joy to the heart,
and good news gives health to the bones.
—Proverbs 15:30

———◆◆◆———

*L*ife affords no greater responsibility,
no greater privilege, than the
raising of the next generation.

———❖———

He decreed statutes ... and established the law ...
which he commanded our forefathers to teach their
children, so the next generation would know them.
—*Psalm 78:5-6*

———❖———

7

*H*aving children makes one
no more a parent than having
a piano makes you a pianist.

With your right hand you save me. The Lord will fulfill
his purpose for me; your love, O Lord, endures forever.
—*Psalm 138:7-8*

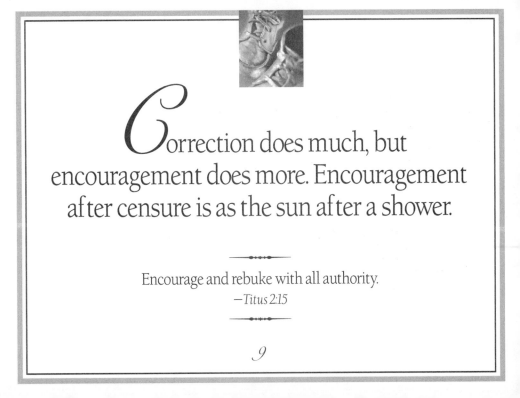

*C*orrection does much, but encouragement does more. Encouragement after censure is as the sun after a shower.

Encourage and rebuke with all authority.
—*Titus 2:15*

*T*here is no finer investment
for any community than
putting milk into babies.

———•◦•———

Our Father in heaven … Give us today our daily bread.
—*Matthew 6:9,11*

———•◦•———

*C*hildren learn what they observe.

These things happened to them as examples—as object
lessons to us—to warn us against doing the same things.
—*1 Corinthians 10:11 TLB*

*W*e must teach our children how
to dream with their eyes open.

———◆———

For as he thinketh in his heart, so is he.
—*Proverbs 23:7 KJV*

———◆———

A child's education should begin
at least one hundred years
before he is born.

Your sons and your daughters shall prophesy, and your young
men shall see visions, and your old men shall dream dreams.

—Acts 2:17 NRSV

---

*E*ach child is an adventure into a better life—an opportunity to change the old pattern and make it new.

Direct my footsteps according to your word.
—*Psalm 119:133*

14

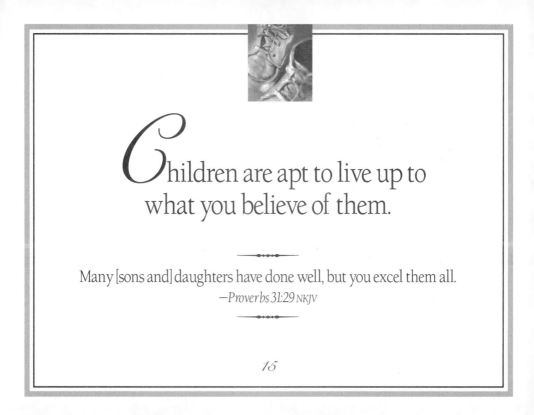

*C*hildren are apt to live up to what you believe of them.

Many [sons and] daughters have done well, but you excel them all.
—*Proverbs 31:29 NKJV*

*W*hen you put faith, hope, and
love together, you can raise
positive kids in a negative world.

God did not give us a spirit of cowardice, but rather
a spirit of power and of love and of self-discipline.

—*2 Timothy 1:7* NRSV

16

*C*hildren have more need of
models than of critics.

She opens her arms to the poor and extends her hands to the needy.
—*Proverbs 31:20*

A baby is something you carry inside you for nine months, in your arms for three years, and in your heart till the day you die.

Lo, children are an heritage of the Lord.
—*Psalm 127:3 KJV*

18

$\mathcal{G}$overn a family as you would cook a small fish—very gently.

Peacemakers who sow in peace raise a harvest of righteousness.
—*James 3:18*

A family is a place where
principles are hammered and
honed on the anvil of everyday living.

———✦———

And David shepherded them with integrity of heart;
with skillful hands he led them.

—Psalm 78:72

———✦———

*C*hildren are the hands by
which we take hold of Heaven.

Because the Lord is my Shepherd, I have everything I need!
—*Psalm 23:1 TLB*

---

*T*o bring up a child in the way
he should go, travel that way
yourself once in awhile.

Love the Lord your God with all your heart and with all your soul and
with all your strength. These commandments that I give you today
are to be upon your hearts. Impress them on your children.

—Deuteronomy 6:5-7

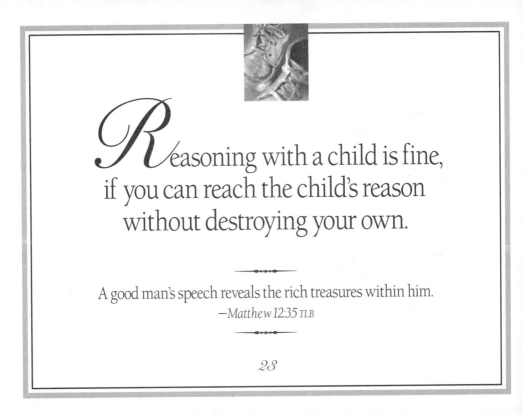

*R*easoning with a child is fine,
if you can reach the child's reason
without destroying your own.

A good man's speech reveals the rich treasures within him.
—*Matthew 12:35 TLB*

*T*here is only one pretty child in the world, and every mother has it.

What a man desires is unfailing love.
—Proverbs 19:22

A young branch takes on
all the bends that one gives to it.

———•◦•———

For when the way is rough, your patience has a chance to grow.
So let it grow, and don't try to squirm out of your problems.

—*James 1:3-4 TLB*

———•◦•———

*O*f all nature's gifts to the human race,
what is sweeter to a man
than his children?

Children are a gift from God; they are his reward.
—*Psalm 127:3 TLB*

---

*F*athers can shape their children's understanding of their mothers by loving them deeply.

Beloved, let us love one another, because love is from God; everyone who loves is born of God and knows God.

—1 John 4:7-8 NRSV

27

Let your children go if you want to keep them.

"So there is hope for your future," declares the Lord.
"Your children will return to their own land."
—*Jeremiah 31:17*

What children hear at home
soon flies abroad.

———✦———

A wise man's heart guides his mouth, and his lips promote instruction.
—*Proverbs 16:23*

———✦———

*W*hen we teach our children properly
in the Word and live the Word before them,
we are fulfilled with beautiful children.

Let the little children come to me, and do not stop them;
for it is to such as these that the kingdom of heaven belongs.
—Matthew 19:14 NRSV

*Y*ou can lead a boy to college, but you cannot make him think.

The hand of the diligent makes rich.
—*Proverbs 10:4* NKJV

*F*or many little girls, life with father is
a dress rehearsal for love and marriage.

———◆◆◆———

A happy heart makes the face cheerful, but heartache crushes the spirit.
—*Proverbs 15:13*

———◆◆◆———

*A*llow children to be happy
their own way; for what better
way will they ever find?

Do not put out the Spirit's fire.
—*1 Thessalonians 5:19*

*T*he more a child becomes aware of
a father's willingness to listen, the
more a father will begin to hear.

Take note of this: Everyone should be quick to listen,
slow to speak and slow to become angry.
—James 1:19

*W*hen you find a spark of grace
in a young heart, kneel down
and blow it into a flame.

The unfolding of your words gives light;
it gives understanding to the simple.

—*Psalm 119:130*

---

*W*hen families fail, society fails.

———◆◆◆◆———

Lord, let our eyes be opened.
—*Matthew 20:33* NRSV

———◆◆◆◆———

*M*y dad and I hunted and fished together. How could I get angry at this man who took the time to be with me?

A wise son heeds his father's instruction.
—*Proverbs 13:1*

37

A father who teaches
his children responsibility
provides them with a fortune.

Listen, my sons, to a father's instruction; pay attention and gain
understanding. I give you sound learning, so do not forsake my teaching.
—*Proverbs 4:1-2*

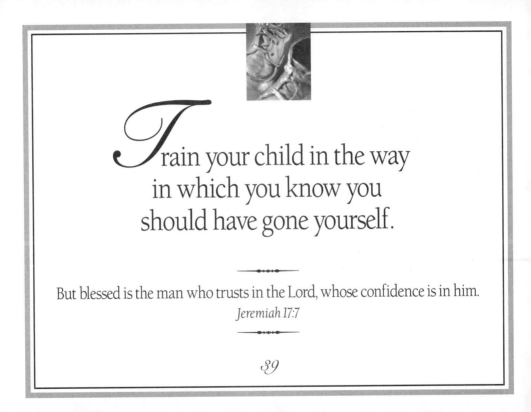

*T*rain your child in the way
in which you know you
should have gone yourself.

But blessed is the man who trusts in the Lord, whose confidence is in him.
Jeremiah 17:7

*C*hildren are God's apostles,
day by day sent forth to preach
of love, and hope, and peace.

We know and rely on the love God has for us. God is love.
Whoever lives in love lives in God, and God in him.
—1 John 4:16

The family is the original Department of Health, Education, and Welfare.

Finally, brothers, whatever is true, whatever is noble, whatever is right, whatever is pure, whatever is lovely, whatever is admirable—if anything is excellent or praiseworthy—think about such things... put it into practice. And the God of peace will be with you.
—*Philippians 4:8-9*

*C*hildren have never been good at listening to elders, but they have never failed to imitate them.

Whatever you do, work at it with all your heart.
—*Colossians 3:23*

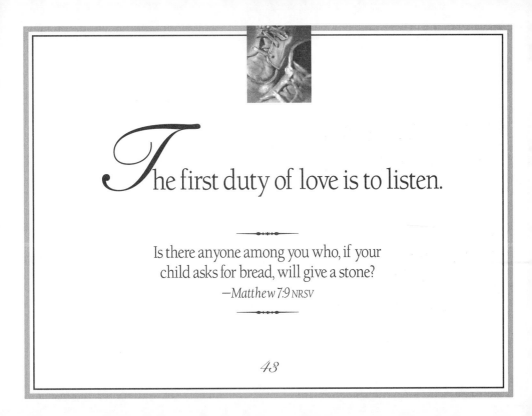

*T*he first duty of love is to listen.

Is there anyone among you who, if your
child asks for bread, will give a stone?
—*Matthew 7:9 NRSV*

There are only two lasting bequests
we can hope to give our children.
One of these is roots. The other, wings.

———◆·:·◆———

Those who hope in the Lord will renew their strength.
They will soar on wings like eagles.
—Isaiah 40:31

———◆·:·◆———

44

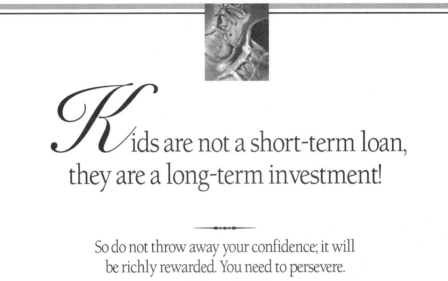

*K*ids are not a short-term loan,
they are a long-term investment!

So do not throw away your confidence; it will
be richly rewarded. You need to persevere.
—*Hebrews 10:35-36*

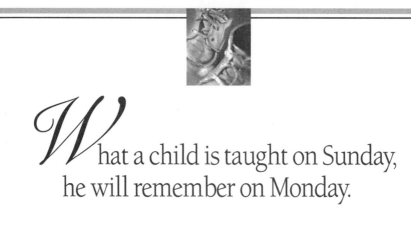

What a child is taught on Sunday, he will remember on Monday.

Apply your mind to instruction and your ear to words of knowledge.
—*Proverbs 23:12* NRSV

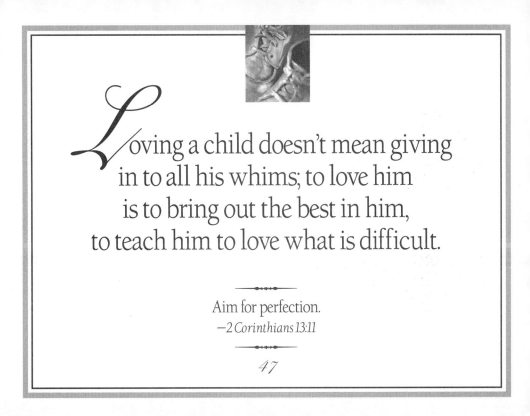

*L*oving a child doesn't mean giving
in to all his whims; to love him
is to bring out the best in him,
to teach him to love what is difficult.

Aim for perfection.
—*2 Corinthians 13:11*

47

A spoiled child never loves its mother.

———◆◇◆———

Discipline your son, and he will give you peace;
he will bring delight to your soul.
—*Proverbs 29:17*

———◆◇◆———

*E*xample is not the main
thing influencing others.
It is the only thing.

The fruit of righteousness will be peace; the effect of
righteousness will be quietness and confidence forever.
—*Isaiah 32:17*

*T*he laughter of a child is
music to a parent's ear.

For the joy of the Lord is your strength.
—*Nehemiah 8:10*

*D*on't limit your child to your own
learning, for he was born in another time.

Then he went down to Nazareth with them and was obedient to them.
But his mother treasured all these things in her heart. And Jesus
grew in wisdom and stature, and in favor with God and men.

—Luke 2:51-52

---

*T*he best brought up children are those who have seen their parents as they are.

Consider it all joy, my brethren, when you encounter various trials,
knowing that the testing of your faith produces endurance.
—*James 1:2-3 NASB*

You grow up the first time
you laugh at yourself.

When a man is gloomy, everything seems to go wrong;
when he is cheerful, everything seems right!
—*Proverbs 15:15* TLB

---

*L*ove is an act of endless forgiveness, a
tender look that becomes a habit.

So he got up and went to his father. But while he was still a long way off,
his father saw him and was filled with compassion for him;
he ran to his son, threw his arms around him and kissed him.

—*Luke 15:20*

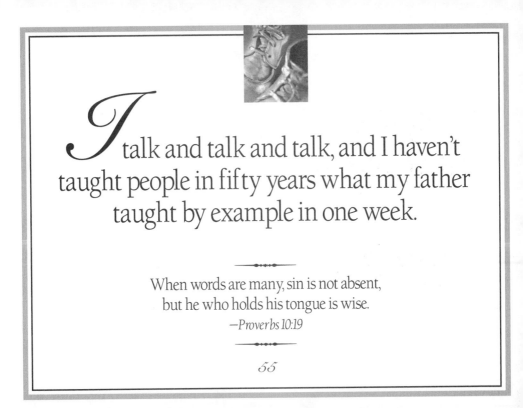

I talk and talk and talk, and I haven't taught people in fifty years what my father taught by example in one week.

When words are many, sin is not absent,
but he who holds his tongue is wise.
—*Proverbs 10:19*

---

*T*he surest way to make it hard for children is to make it easy for them.

Being punished isn't enjoyable while it is happening—it hurts! But afterwards we can see the result, a quiet growth in grace and character.
—*Hebrews 12:11* TLB

---

*Y*ou don't raise heroes, you raise sons. And if you treat them like sons, they'll turn out to be heroes, even if it's just in your own eyes.

As a father has compassion on his children, so the Lord has compassion on those who fear him.

—*Psalm 103:13*

*T*he most important thing is
not so much that every child should
be taught, as that every child should
be given the wish to learn.

———

Seek, and ye shall find; knock, and it shall be opened unto you.
—*Matthew 7:7 KJV*

———

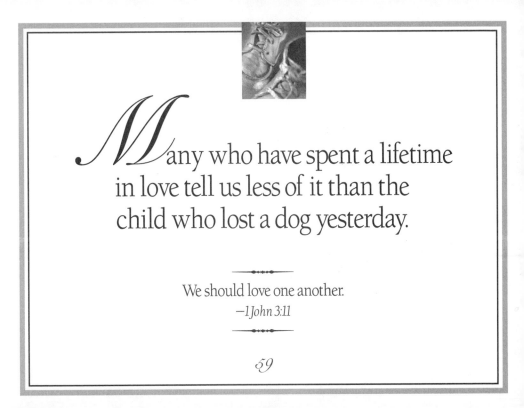

*M*any who have spent a lifetime in love tell us less of it than the child who lost a dog yesterday.

We should love one another.
—*1 John 3:11*

59

*W*e discover our parents when we become parents ourselves.

Grandchildren are the crown of the aged,
and the glory of children is their parents.
—*Proverbs 17:6 NRSV*

A child's hand in yours—
what tenderness it arouses, what power
it conjures. You are instantly the very
touchstone of wisdom and strength.

The purposes of a man's heart are deep waters,
but a man of understanding draws them out.
—*Proverbs 20:5*

61

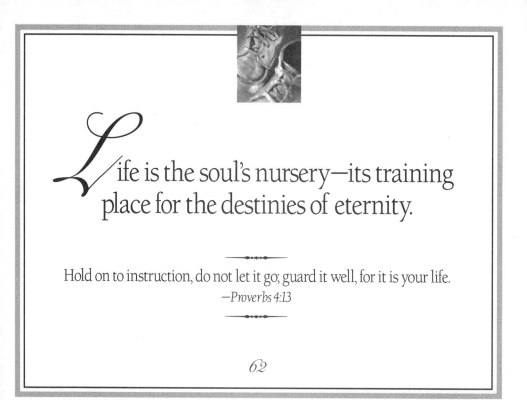

*L*ife is the soul's nursery—its training place for the destinies of eternity.

Hold on to instruction, do not let it go; guard it well, for it is your life.
—*Proverbs 4:13*

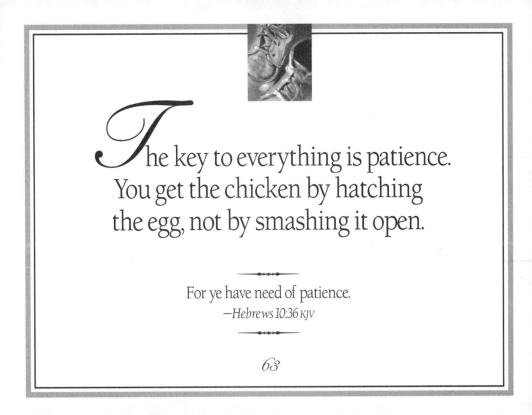

$\mathcal{T}$he key to everything is patience.
You get the chicken by hatching
the egg, not by smashing it open.

For ye have need of patience.
—*Hebrews 10:36* KJV

63

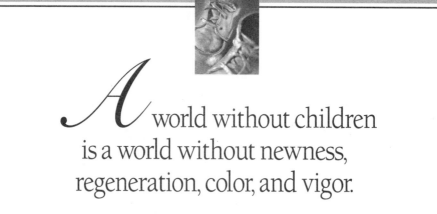

A world without children
is a world without newness,
regeneration, color, and vigor.

Unless you change and become like children,
you will never enter the kingdom of heaven.
—*Matthew 18:3 NRSV*

*T*hat energy which makes a child hard to manage is the energy that afterwards makes him a manager of life.

Therefore encourage one another and build each other up.
—1 Thessalonians 5:11

65

When you're dealing with a child,
keep your wits about you,
and sit on the floor.

Make the most of every opportunity.
—*Colossians 4:5*

66

*C*hildren have to be educated, but
they have also to be left
to educate themselves.

My son, do not forget my teaching, but keep my commands in your heart.
—*Proverbs 3:1*

The tongue is the deadliest of all blunt instruments.

———◆·❖·◆———

Fathers, do not provoke your children, or they may lose heart.
—*Colossians 3:21* NRSV

———◆·❖·◆———

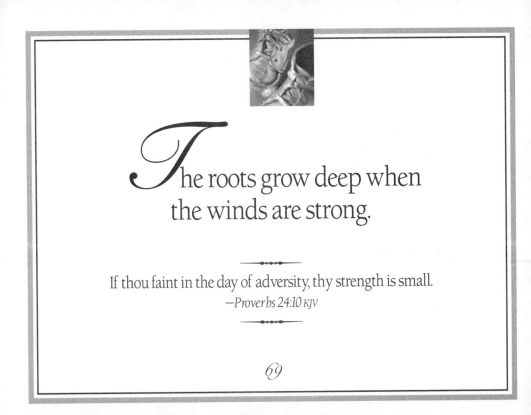

The roots grow deep when the winds are strong.

If thou faint in the day of adversity, thy strength is small.
—*Proverbs 24:10* KJV

*T*he most important thing a father
can do for his children
is to love their mother.

———◆◆◆———

Where your treasure is, there your heart will be also.
—Matthew 6:21 NRSV

———◆◆◆———

$\mathcal{B}$e not angry that you cannot make others as you wish them to be, since you cannot make yourself as you wish to be.

It is better to be slow-tempered than famous; it is better to have self-control than to control an army.

—*Proverbs 16:32 TLB*

71

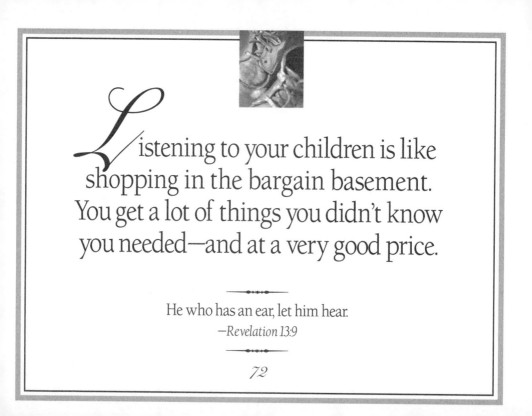

*L*istening to your children is like shopping in the bargain basement. You get a lot of things you didn't know you needed—and at a very good price.

He who has an ear, let him hear.
—Revelation 13:9

72

$\mathcal{T}$here is no education like adversity.

A just man falleth seven times, and riseth up again.
—*Proverbs 24:16* KJV

*L*ife's aspirations come in
the guise of children.

May the Lord bless you ... all the days of your life ...
and may you live to see your children's children.
—*Psalm 128:5-6*

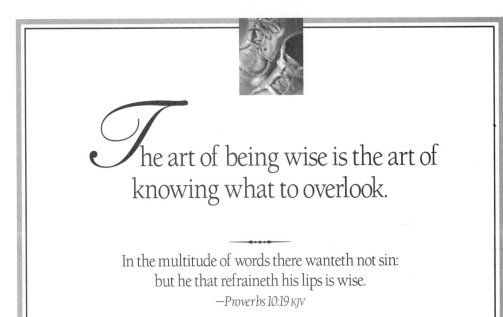

The art of being wise is the art of knowing what to overlook.

In the multitude of words there wanteth not sin:
but he that refraineth his lips is wise.
—*Proverbs 10:19 KJV*

---

*C*hildren can stand vast
amounts of sternness. They rather expect
to be wrong, and are quite used to being
punished. It is injustice, inequity, and
inconsistency that kills them.

———◆◆◆———

Don't fail to correct your children; discipline won't hurt them!
—*Proverbs 23:13 TLB*

———◆◆◆———

*T*he young have no depth perception
in time. Ten years back or
ten years forward is an eternity.

Where there is no vision, the people perish.
—*Proverbs 29:18 KJV*

*G*od will not demand more from
you as a parent than what
He will help you do.

For with God nothing shall be impossible.
—Luke 1:37 KJV

78

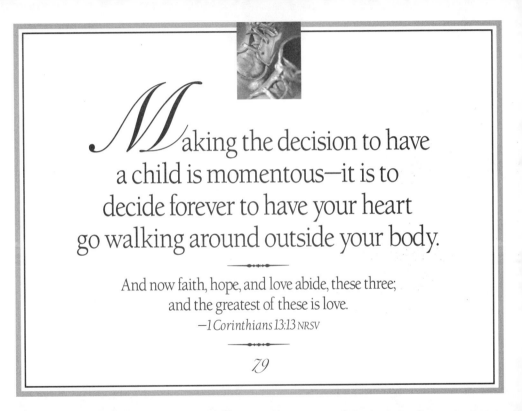

Making the decision to have
a child is momentous—it is to
decide forever to have your heart
go walking around outside your body.

And now faith, hope, and love abide, these three;
and the greatest of these is love.
—*1 Corinthians 13:13 NRSV*

If it was going to be easy to raise kids, it never would have started with something called labor.

He gives us more grace.
—James 4:6

*C*hildren find comfort in flaws, ignorance, and insecurities similar to their own. I love my mother for letting me see hers.

"They will be mine," says the Lord Almighty, "in the day when I make up my treasured possession."
—*Malachi 3:17*

*L*ife isn't a matter of milestones,
but of moments.

But encourage one another daily, as long as it is still called Today.
—*Hebrews 3:13*

We can do no great things—only small things with great love.

Let all that you do be done in love.
—*1 Corinthians 16:14* NRSV

*I*t's the three pairs of eyes that mothers have to have
... one pair that sees through closed doors ... another
in the back of her head ... and, of course, the ones in
front that can look at a child when he goofs up
and reflect "I understand and I love you"
without so much as uttering a word.

Her children arise and call her blessed; her husband also, and he praises her.
—*Proverbs 31:28*

The mother's heart is the child's schoolroom.

She speaks with wisdom, and faithful instruction is on her tongue.
—*Proverbs 31:26*

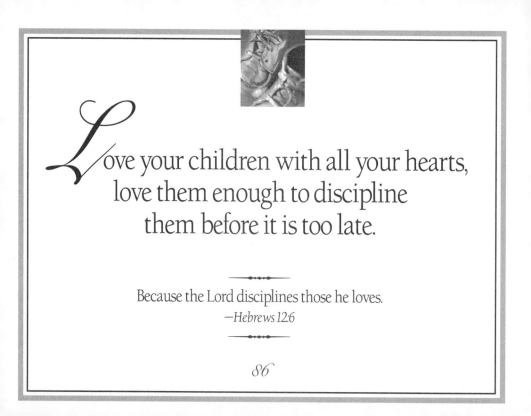

*L*ove your children with all your hearts,
love them enough to discipline
them before it is too late.

Because the Lord disciplines those he loves.
—Hebrews 12:6

*A*t every step the child should be allowed to meet the real experiences of life; the thorns should never be plucked from their roses.

For God hath not given us the spirit of fear; but of power, and of love, and of a sound mind.

—*2 Timothy 1:7 KJV*

87

*C*hildren begin by loving their parents.
As they grow older, they judge them.
Sometimes they forgive them.

By wisdom a house is built, and through understanding it is established;
through knowledge its rooms are filled with rare and beautiful treasures.
—*Proverbs 24:3-4*

*T*he best things you can give children,
next to good habits, are good memories.

I remember the days of long ago; I meditate on all your
works and consider what your hands have done.
—*Psalm 143:5*

---

*R*emember, when they have a tantrum, don't have one of your own.

Those with good sense are slow to anger,
and it is their glory to overlook an offense.
—*Proverbs 19:11* NRSV

_T_ believe the child should be taught from the very first that the whole world is his world, that adult and child share one world, that all generations are needed.

Those who are wise will shine like the brightness of the heavens.
—_Daniel 12:3_

*C*hildren are unpredictable.
You never know what inconsistency
they're going to catch you in next.

Reckless words pierce like a sword, but
the tongue of the wise brings healing.
—*Proverbs 12:18*

*N*ever show a child what he cannot see ...
While you are thinking about what
will be useful to him when he is older,
talk to him of what he can use now.

A fool uttereth all his mind: but a wise man keepeth it in till afterwards.
—*Proverbs 29:11 KJV*

93

*L*et thy child's first lesson be obedience,
and the second will be what thou wilt.

Whoever loves discipline loves knowledge,
but he who hates correction is stupid.

—*Proverbs 12:1*

---

*P*arents who are afraid to put
their foot down usually have
children who step on their toes.

He who heeds discipline shows the way to life, but
whoever ignores correction leads others astray.
—*Proverbs 10:17*

---

*Y*ou are the bow from which your children, as living arrows, are sent forth.

I have no greater joy than this, to hear that my children are walking in the truth.
—3 John 1:4 NRSV

96

A torn jacket is soon mended, but hard words bruise the heart of a child.

An angry man stirs up dissension, and
a hot-tempered one commits many sins.
—*Proverbs 29:22*

*I*t is almost always through fear of being criticized that people tell lies.

An honest answer is like a kiss on the lips.
—Proverbs 24:26

*T*he child becomes largely
what he is taught, hence we must
watch what we teach and how we live.

Teach them [God's commandments] to your children,
talking about them when you are at home and when you
are away, when you lie down and when you rise. So that
your days and the days of your children may be multiplied.

—*Deuteronomy 11:19,21* NRSV

What we desire our children to become,
we must endeavor to be before them.

Therefore be imitators of God as dear children. And walk in love,
as Christ also has loved us and given Himself for us, an offering
and a sacrifice to God for a sweet-smelling aroma.

—*Ephesians 5:1-2* NKJV

---

*I*t is not enough for parents to understand children. They must accord children the privilege of understanding them.

Be very careful, then, how you live—not as unwise but as wise, making the most of every opportunity.
—*Ephesians 5:15-16*

101

*U*pon our children—how they are
taught—rests the fate, or fortune,
of tomorrow's world.

And having done everything...stand firm.
—*Ephesians 6:13* NRSV

Respect the child. Be not too much his parent. Trespass not on his solitude.

The Lord is compassionate and gracious, slow to anger, abounding in love.
—*Psalm 103:8*

103

*I*t is better to bind your children
to you by a feeling of respect, and
by gentleness, than by fear.

A word to you parents. Don't keep on scolding and nagging your children,
making them angry and resentful. Rather, bring them up with the loving
discipline the Lord himself approves, with suggestions and godly advice.

—*Ephesians 6:4 TLB*

*W*e must not educate our children in order to send them into the world as finished products, but as a person well begun.

Train a child in the way he should go, and when he is old he will not turn from it.

—*Proverbs 22:6*

105

$\mathcal{T}$each your children not to follow the whims of adolescent society. They can lead, or they can follow. It's better to lead.

Teach these things. Don't let anyone look down on you because you are young, but set an example for the believers in speech, in life, in love, in faith and in purity.

—1 Timothy 4:11-12

---

*E*ven at fifty years of age, people will remember and be guided by that which was taught in childhood. It's an awesome thought.

Teach a child to choose the right path, and
when he is older he will remain upon it.
—*Proverbs 22:6 TLB*

---

*L*ove your children unselfishly.
That's hard but it's the only way.

There is no fear in love, but perfect love casts out fear.
—*1 John 4:18* NRSV

---

*Y*ou cannot teach a child to take care of himself unless you will let him try to take care of himself. He will make mistakes; and out of those mistakes will come wisdom.

Perseverance must finish its work so that you may
be mature and complete, not lacking anything.

—James 1:4

---

*W*e are far more liable to catch the vices than the virtues of our associates.

Do not be misled: "Bad company corrupts good character."
—*1 Corinthians 15:33*

*T*each a child to trust in God, not
the morning headlines.

Trust in the Lord forever, for the Lord, the Lord, is the Rock eternal.
—*Isaiah 26:4*

A child tells in the street what its father and mother say in the home.

For the value of wisdom is far above rubies;
nothing can be compared with it.

—*Proverbs 8:11* TLB

*T*n case of doubt, it is better to say too little than too much.

For everything there is a season ... a time to keep silence, and a time to speak.
—*Ecclesiastes 3:1,7* NRSV

To instill a healthy prayer life in your children, pray yourself.

Evening, and morning, and at noon, will I pray, and cry aloud: and he shall hear my voice.

—*Psalm 55:17 KJV*

114

*C*hildren are natural mimics,
imitating your words and deeds.

———

Show me your faith without deeds, and
I will show you my faith by what I do.
—James 2:18

———

*I*t is the child's love of his parents that makes him want to adopt their best traits and learn the qualities they urge upon him.

For I have given you an example, that ye should do as I have done to you.
—*John 13:15 KJV*

*C*hildren as a rule do not want
to be indulged. They want
to be responsible.

Even a child is known by his actions, by
whether his conduct is pure and right.
—*Proverbs 20:11*

117

$\mathcal{T}$o understand your parents' love
you must raise children yourself.

For you know that we dealt with each of you as a father deals
with his own children, encouraging, comforting and
urging you to live lives worthy of God.
—*1 Thessalonians 2:11-12*

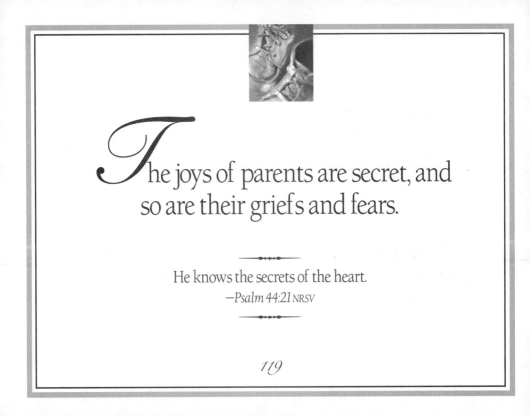

The joys of parents are secret, and so are their griefs and fears.

He knows the secrets of the heart.
—*Psalm 44:21* NRSV

*T*t is only by obedience that
we understand the teaching of God.

Children, obey your parents; this is the right thing to do because God has
placed them in authority over you. Honor your father and mother.
—*Ephesians 6:1-2 TLB*

A man who gives his children habits of industry provides for them better than by giving them a fortune.

The sleep of a labouring man is sweet.
—*Ecclesiastes 5:12 KJV*

*C*hildren seldom misquote you. In fact, they usually repeat word for word what you shouldn't have said.

In everything set them an example by doing what is good. In your teaching show integrity, seriousness and soundness of speech.

—*Titus 2:7-8*

*C*herish all your happy moments.

———◆◆◆———

A merry heart maketh a cheerful countenance:
but by sorrow of the heart the spirit is broken.
—*Proverbs 15:13 KJV*

———◆◆◆———

 $\mathcal{L}$ook for a lovely thing and
you will find it.

Be content with such things as ye have.
—*Hebrews 13:5 KJV*

124

*F*irst keep peace within yourself, then you can also bring peace to others.

I have stilled and quieted my soul.
—*Psalm 131:2*

The most beautiful action in the world is to love. The second most beautiful is to give.

The light in the eyes [of him whose heart is joyful]
rejoices the hearts of others.
—*Proverbs 15:30* AMP

$\mathcal{B}$lessed is the man who keeps in touch with his child's heart.

A patient man has great understanding.
—*Proverbs 14:29*

*D*irect your efforts more to preparing youth for the path and less preparing the path for youth.

Now devote your heart and soul to seeking the Lord your God.

—1 Chronicles 22:19

---

*P*rayer is simple, as simple as a child making known its wants to its parents.

By day the Lord directs his love, at night his song
is with me—a prayer to the God of my life.
—*Psalm 42:8*

*W*hatever you do, put romance and enthusiasm into the life of your children.

Love each other as I have loved you.
—John 15:12

$\mathcal{A}$lways laugh when you can.
It is cheap medicine.

———•◦•———

Be joyful always.
—1 Thessalonians 5:16

———•◦•———

*O*for a thousand tongues to sing
my great Redeemer's praise!

My heart is steadfast, O God; I will sing and make music with all my soul.
—*Psalm 108:1*

*I*t's never too late to have
a happy childhood.

A merry heart doeth good like a medicine:
but a broken spirit drieth the bones.
—*Proverbs 17:22 KJV*

133

*T*he only power which can resist the power of fear is the power of love.

When I am afraid, I will trust in you.
—*Psalm 56:3*

The soul is healed by being
with children.

Sing to him a new song; play skillfully, and shout for joy.
—*Psalm 33:3*

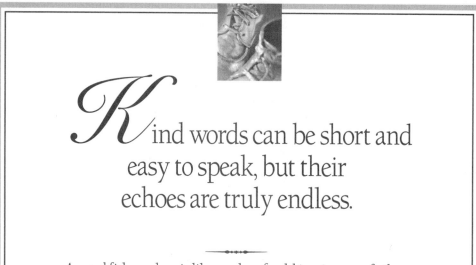

*K*ind words can be short and
easy to speak, but their
echoes are truly endless.

A word fitly spoken is like apples of gold in pictures of silver.
—*Proverbs 25:11 KJV*

*T*he best thing about the future is that it comes only one day at a time.

When my spirit grows faint within me, it is you who know my way.
—*Psalm 142:3*

137

*T*t is only with the heart that one can see rightly; what is essential is invisible to the eye.

My son, give me thine heart.
—*Proverbs 23:26 KJV*

*I*f you judge people, you have
no time to love them.

—◆◆◆—

Judge not, and ye shall not be judged: condemn not,
and ye shall not be condemned.

—Luke 6:37 KJV

—◆◆◆—

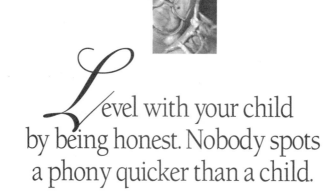

*L*evel with your child
by being honest. Nobody spots
a phony quicker than a child.

Provide things honest in the sight of all men.
—Romans 12:17 KJV

140

I do the very best I know how, the very best I can.

Let your light shine before men, that they may see
your good deeds and praise your Father in heaven.
—*Matthew 5:16*

*T*rouble knocked at the door, but hearing a laugh within hurried away.

If God be for us, who can be against us?
—*Romans 8:31 KJV*

---

*M*ake that possible for me which is impossible by nature.

Anything is possible if you have faith.
—*Mark 9:23* TLB

143

*P*ray daily for your children and
don't be afraid to let them
see you on your knees.

We always thank God for all of you, mentioning you in our prayers.
—*1 Thessalonians 1:2*

---

*A*ll kids are gifted; some just open
their packages earlier than others.

———◆◆◆———

Don't show favoritism.
—*James 2:1*

———◆◆◆———

145

*C*onfidence, like art, never comes
from having all the answers; it comes
from being open to all the questions.

———•◦•◦•———

Faith is being sure of what we hope
for and certain of what we do not see.
—*Hebrews 11:1*

———•◦•◦•———

146

*W*e need four hugs a day for survival.
We need eight hugs a day for maintenance.
We need twelve hugs a day for growth.

———•‖•———

May the Lord make your love increase and
overflow for each other and for everyone else.
—*1 Thessalonians 3:12*

———•‖•———

*E*ach day of our lives we make deposits in the memory banks of our children.

The just man walketh in his integrity: his children are blessed after him.
—Proverbs 20:7 KJV

148

*O*ur greatest glory is not in never failing
but in rising up every time we fail.

Blessed is the man who perseveres under trial, because when
he has stood the test, he will receive the crown of life.

—James 1:12

149

*W*e worry about what a child
will be tomorrow, yet we forget
that he is someone today.

———◆◆◆———

Don't be anxious about tomorrow. God will take
care of your tomorrow too. Live one day at a time.
—*Matthew 6:34 TLB*

———◆◆◆———

*C*leaning your house while your kids are still growing is like shoveling the walk before it stops snowing.

For I have learned, in whatsoever state I am, therewith to be content. I can do all things through Christ which strengtheneth me.
—*Philippians 4:11,13 KJV*

---

*W*here there is great love
there are always miracles.

———◆◆◆———

The Lord is my light and my salvation.
—*Psalm 27:1*

———◆◆◆———

152

$\mathcal{M}$ost troubles are imaginary: what you think are huge clouds in the sky may be nothing more than dust on your eyelashes.

Cast your cares on the Lord and he will sustain
you; he will never let the righteous fall.
—*Psalm 55:22*

---

*O*ut of the mouths of babes come words
we shouldn't have said in the first place.

For out of the abundance of the heart the mouth speaketh.
—*Matthew 12:34 KJV*

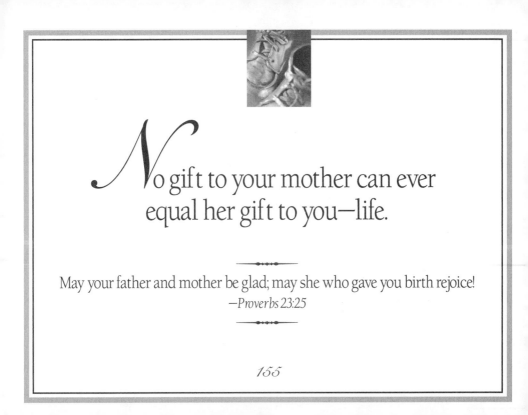

*N*o gift to your mother can ever
equal her gift to you—life.

May your father and mother be glad; may she who gave you birth rejoice!
—*Proverbs 23:25*

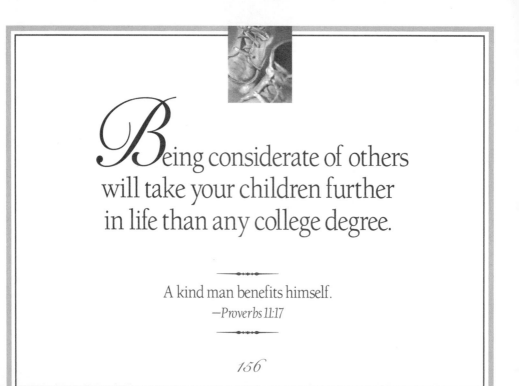

$\mathcal{B}$eing considerate of others
will take your children further
in life than any college degree.

———◆•◆◆•◆———

A kind man benefits himself.
—*Proverbs 11:17*

———◆•◆◆•◆———

156

To show a child what once
delighted you, to find the child's delight
added to your own, this is happiness.

A happy heart makes the face cheerful.
—*Proverbs 15:13*

157

$\mathcal{A}$cknowledgments

The publisher would like to honor and acknowledge the following people for the quotes used in this book:

Frank Clark (4), Robert Gardner (5), Dr. Henker (6), C. Everett Koop (7), Michael Levine (8), Johann Wolfgang von Goethe (9), Winston Churchill (10), Dorothy Knolte (11), Harry Edwards (12), Oliver Wendell Holmes (13), Hubert H. Humphrey (14), Lady Bird Johnson (15), Zig Ziglar (16), Joseph Joebert (17), Mary Mason (18), Charles Swindoll (20,69,148), Josh Billings (22), John Mason Brown (23), Cicero (26), Dr. James Dobson (27,37,64,106,107), Samuel Johnson (28,33), Thomas Fuller, M.D. (29), Pat Harrison (30), Elbert Hubbard (31), David Jeremiah (32), Gordon MacDonald (34), Charles Spurgeon (35,39), Dan Quayle (36), James Russell Lowell (40), William J. Bennett (41), James Baldwin (42), Paul Tillich (43), Hodding Carter (44), Welsh Proverb (46), Nadia Boulanger (47), Sir Henry Taylor (48), Albert Schweitzer (49), George Bernard Shaw (52), Ethel Barrymore (53), Peter Ustinov (54), Mario Cuomo (55), Eleanor Roosevelt (56), Walter M. Schirra, Sr. (57), John Lubbock (58), Thornton Wilder (59), Marjorie Holmes (61), William Makepeace Thackeray (62), Arnold Glasgow (63), Henry Ward Beecher (65,85,109), Austin O'Malley (66), Abbe Dimnet (67), Theodore M. Hesburgh (70), Thomas à Kempis (71,125,143), Benjamin Disraeli (73), Rabindranath Tagore (74), William James (75), Robert F. Capon (76), Robert C. Alberts (77), Elizabeth Stone (79), Erma Bombeck (81,84), Rose Fitzgerald (82), Mother Teresa (83,136,139), Lavina Christensen Fugal (86), Ellen Key (87), Oscar Wilde (88), Sydney J. Harris (89), Dr. Judith Kariansky (90), Pearl S. Buck (91), Franklin P. Jones (92), Jean Jacques Rousseau (93), Benjamin Franklin (94,142), Chinese proverb (95,153), Kahlil Gibran (96), Henry Wadsworth Longfellow (97), Paul Tournier (98), Jane Adams (99), Andrew Combe (100), Milton Sapirstein (101), B.C. Forbes (102), Ralph Waldo Emerson (103,149), Terence (104), Sr. Angela Boyd (105), Barbara Bush (108), Denis Diderot (110), Thomas Jefferson (113), Morton Hunt (116), Hannah Lees (117), Francis Bacon (119), Oswald Chambers (120,129), Richard Whately (121), Margaret Moore (123), Sara Teasdale (124), Bertha Von Suttner (126), Benjamin Barr Lindsey (128), Margaret MacDonald (130), Lord Byron (131), Charles Wesley (132), Tom Robbins (133), Alan Stewart Paton (134), Fyodor Dostoyevski (135), Abraham Lincoln (137,141), Antoine de Saint-Exupéry (138), Mary MacCracken (140), Michael Carr (145), Earl Gray Stevens (146), Virginia Satir (147), Stacia Tauscher (150), Phyllis Diller (151), Willa Cather (152), Marian Wright Edelman (156), J.B. Priestley (157).

Additional copies of this book and other titles in the *God's Little Instruction Book* series are available from your local bookstore.

God's Little Instruction Book
God's Little Instruction Book for Mom
God's Little Instruction Book for Dad
God's Little Instruction Book for Students
God's Little Instruction Book for Graduates
God's Little Instruction Book for Teachers

If you have enjoyed this book, or if it has impacted your life, we would like to hear from you. Please contact us at:

Honor Books
Department E
P.O. Box 55388
Tulsa, Oklahoma 74155
Or by e-mail at info@honorbooks.com